FROM MY
Journal
NOTES

ALL OF THAT
WAS FOR THIS

IVY GRAY

From My Journal Notes

From My Journal Notes

Copyright © 2023 by Ivy Gray

Published by Grace 4 Purpose, Publishing Co. LLC

ISBN: 979-8-9879298-7-2

Editing by: Grace 4 Purpose, Publishing Co. LLC & Parris Baker, PhD.

Book cover design by Untouchable Designz and Consulting

Cover Photo by: Dante Bland LLC

Printed and bound in the United States of America

DEDICATION

This book is dedicated to God and my attempt to acknowledge how He's changed my life. I would also like to dedicate this book to everyone who has played a role in molding me into who I am today. Lastly, to my daughter, Micah, the better version of me.

TABLE OF CONTENTS

Prelude

*U*ltimately, quite often life is viewed with the eyes of opposing extremes: What we have and what we don't have, who we are and who we are not and the transition between the former and the latter. This book is my point of view of how mental health, emotional intelligence, and faith has transformed my mind from one state of being to another. The change of mind has unlocked the door to the change in my quality of life. You are about to read my diary. You are about to read what's meant when said, "I should write a book about my life." This is a small peak into the window of the beginning of my life, not who I am now

There was once a time I thought I'd lose my mind. The same holds true for you. Will you say it aloud, or must I do it for you? We all have stories that go untold, the difference between us is I'm a little more bold. Read until the end because when you're done the beginning of your own story would have begun. Don't read it though with a heart to judge, but it may explain our encounters begrudged.

Introduction

IN THE DARK OF THE TUNNEL BUT I THINK

I SEE A LIGHT

I'll never trust again, nor will I ever be vulnerable without purpose. After what you've done to me my mind has transcended above the average thoughts of love. I love people, the many different versions of God's image. I'll get to know you, the good, the bad and indifferent but never again will you know me. You won't know me, so you won't hurt me. You won't know what makes me sad, my fears or what makes me cry. You'll only know me by my acts of love. God is love. His residence is within me. All I can give is the love that you need when you need it without motive or need for reciprocity. When I'm depleted, I'll only be restored from above. When I say you, I'm speaking to the you who knows what has been done to me and the "you" that comes along the way. I speak from a spectrum of healing not at the beginning or the end but midway through. The more I write, the more I heal. The more that you read; your mind, spirit, and soul will discover your own path of healing. I expose my truths to give you the courage to face yours.

"I'll never trust again nor be vulnerable again" sounds poetic right? Your mind is telling you to build a wall of protection but really you're building a prison. Self-sabotage. Mental and emotional suicide. Telling you that a certain part of your life is hopeless or not worth living but in actuality it's the truth that sets you free.

Have I lost my mind, or have I loosed it? What do you do with trauma? Does it truly go away or is it displaced? It chases you down, looms like a shadow that shades the identity of who you truly are. This is merely my opinion personal not professional, but I believe that you're only traumatized once. Then it goes with you and grows with you Re-presenting itself over and over again each time with a different face or place until finally, you detach it from your life.

Regardless of the many places that I've lived and traveled, the things I've seen and heard and the people that I've met The most constant part of my life has been God's presence. I've seen and felt him everywhere, that's why I know that he is omnipresent. Many years I questioned, why? why! why?

and the answer finally came: For discipline, growth, development and to reach identity. Remember earlier when I told you that trauma looms like a shadow that shades the

identity of who you truly are? You are already YOU, but it will take discipline, growth and development to uncover and rediscover yourself. I need my faith to survive, for me it is my lifeline.

In my developmental years when my personality, morals, and character was being molded and the way that I view the world was being shaped, I did not get the assurance and validation that I needed to feel that I mattered or was loved. Over time, it formed a trauma called rejection and abandonment. In my home it was always made known that "once you turn 18, you're grown, and you're gone" and from that came this poem:

"Home is where the heart is"

That saying is untrue.

Home is wherever open arms lovingly embrace you.

Home is where those loving arms gently guide you in and warms the chilled frost on your hands although I'm full of sin.

But wait too long in that embrace and I overhear

Those arms of love have turned to hate and dangers

very near.

Decide to hide or to abide

you've heard them plan out your demise.

I've always been searching for an external place to call home not knowing that what I was really looking for was a sense of belonging, to love and to be loved without fear of it being retracted. Growing up in my household, we lacked oneness, there wasn't any coming together or bonding. No expression of emotions and no affection. At least, not that I can remember. I'm trying hard to remember. My father, his struggle with addictions to drugs and alcohol always ended in physical violence. I remember a game that we used to play. It would be whatever time of night, but always after bedtime. We'd hear my father come crashing into the front door sometimes he had been gone for days, and other times it would have been that he left earlier in the day. None the less when he was home, there was fear and violence. He'd always hurt my mom. Drag her through the house by her legs, beat her, pin her down to do obscene things and venom always foamed out of his mouth. I laid in my room listening both intently and quietly and I imagine that my brothers in their room did the same. I'm unsure of who came up with the game but it was decided. On nights when my father came home, we hide, seek, and run. In the pitch-black dark we'd slide out of our beds and maneuver about the apartment around his noises and thrashing into things. It was easily done because, he never had his wits about him when he was under the influence.

We never usually made it to the door at the same time but when we did we'd run outside to the car to sleep for the night. One particular night, I was moving too slowly, so in order to not be discovered, instead of heading for the front door, I had to retreat to my mother's room. I postured myself in the corner of the room by the closet door when suddenly, faster than I could blink, my father came charging towards me like a bull. The next thing I saw were stars twinkling in my right eye and pain so bad that I took my breath away before finally I was able to let out an agonized scream. My father had punched me dead center in my eye. Bullseye. When he realized that it was me his response was. "Oh, I'm sorry Ivy, I thought you was your mama." I think that was the end of our game nights.

After many more times of running and hiding my mother finally had the strength to gather my brothers and I and leave. I would not have known what all went into that action until I had to do it myself later in life. Leave. One day she met a man. She liked him more than he liked her from what I could see, but he also really liked me. He taught me that my body could do things that I at the time did not know it was supposed to do but the biggest thing he taught me was to keep secrets. He taught me to let things happen to me that were not supposed to happen. I taught myself to let my mind wander and detach from the things that I'm uncomfortable with. I could take my mind into an imaginary land of exploration of thoughts, almost able to completely forget what was real in the moment. Later in my life he apologized for his wrongdoing. I have accepted it.

I had plentiful opportunities to use my ability to be quiet and keep secrets. When the babysitter's son fondled me I kept quiet. One day, my mother dropped us off to be babysit by a woman that she said was family. I didn't exactly know who they were then and I only vaguely remember now. What I do remember is being content to sit in front of the box television with my brothers' watching cartoons. The adult was gone and we were left with her teenagers. Two girls and a boy. The girls came to get me to play and have girl time after pretending to play with me for a short time , they took me to the garage, had me pull down my pants and lay on my stomach.

They left me. He was there with me. I remember the cold hard concrete and the pressure of what he was doing to me. I remember the pain. He kindly and gently said to me, "Please be quiet, I'm almost done, here eat these potato chips, they taste good." The girls appeared in the doorway! I was happy to see them thinking they were coming to save me and that all of this was a mistake. They stood watch. They were coming to guard the actions of my abuser not to save me. At that moment I was happy that I'd learned the art of detachment. I lay there eating the soggy potato chips wet and salty from the droplets of my silent tears.

When it was over they ran me a bubble bath and gave me rubber ducks to play with. imagine the confusion of mind. My playing days were over. They cleaned and dressed me, putting me back in front of the television with my brothers, they asked where I'd been. "Playing with the girls" was my answer as I immersed myself into the world of cartoons.

I told you earlier that in my home, "Once you're eighteen you're grown and gone." By that time, I had already moved to a northern city. By the age of eighteen I was already a fighter. I lived with a woman and her two sons that made me feel everything but welcomed. By night, I hear her talking about me on the telephone, how raggedy, pitiful, useless and helpless I was. How she was a good Christian to take me in. I wish she knew that Her walls were thin and that the room she put in next to hers shared a wall. Maybe she would have spoken more softly. By day, the two who lived in the basement would plot on my demise, they were planning to have their way with me. Every morning, they would twist and jiggle my doorknob. It was always locked. They also didn't know that I slept with a kitchen knife under my pillow and under my mattress at all times. One morning, we were ready to execute a new plan. I lay in bed with my hands propped behind my bed listening to the plan. This house had very thin walls. Their voices carried up through the floor as they decided to use a butter knife to unlock my door. Don't bring a butter knife to a steak knife fight I thought laughing to myself. They came upstairs, I stood by the door waiting, ready. Which was victim and which was the prey? They door handle jiggled and the lock turned. The door opened. I turned into a maniac lashing my knife through the air as they retreated.

What does home mean to you? How would you define it? I was looking for a "place" to call home before I realized that home is a feeling. For me, home feels like coming in from being out in the cold on a winter's day. When I open the door the heat rushes to my face. I smell a candle burning or whatever's prepared for dinner. I remove my coat, gloves, and boots and my mind releases the cold and the cares of whatever I did before this moment. I'm home.

Morals, values, characteristics and the core of who you are is made at home, but it is also the breeding place for trauma. As the world expands beyond your home life, both the things that you were fond of and the things that lacked, you try to recreate in the world outside of home. If you lack the discipline and approval of a father, which represents authority, you look for discipline from other forms of authority in your behavior choices. or approval from other forms of authority by means of accomplishments. When lacking the nurturing of a mother you seek to be nurtured by someone or something else and if all else fails and in combination with the other two you try to recreate it within yourself.

Maybe, I shouldn't allude to knowing your thoughts, or picking apart your brain, or performing open surgery on your heart. Who am I to say that you can handle all that pain? Stand behind the observation glass and I'll take that role. The surgeon will cut me open and you will see firsthand what unfolds. The infection inside is purulent and can no longer hide. The surgeon says to you behold all of this mess inside. Then I'll receive that antidote to finally make me clean and he'll look to you behind the looking glass and say you're next, there is no fee. The antidote is free.

I interviewed a few men and women and asked if they learned discipline/accomplishment from their fathers or a father figure and if they received the type of nurturing that was needed from their mother or a mother figure.. Everyone offered honest answers to those questions. However, as I probed some answers were followed by offense and others were able to answer with a clear conscience. The difference came from their individual position of healing or lack of. Those who haven't internally dealt with the issues with their upbringing displayed both guarded posture and tone. Some even began to fidget, subconsciously wrapping their arms around themselves (guarding) and creating physical distance between me and them. They began to speak faster, harsher and trip over words while displaying false confidence and false dismissive word choices to try to prove detachment from that part of themselves.

In contrast, those who have dealt internally with their upbringing answered with more ease and patience with a relaxed disposition. The questions, although the same did not trigger negative reactions. Instead of detachment they had been able to "move on", outgrown or maybe even evolve from that segment of time in their lives. You cannot heal what you hide. How can you expect to cross the bridge to the other side of healing if you won't go near it? Healed wounds no longer hurt. Therefore, offense is a sign of an unhealed wound.

It just so happens that the latter were people of faith. They had secured a relationship with God that acted as a cushion between them and their pain. Faith hadn't stopped the blow, but it softened it. I personally believe that faith covers offense. Not to say that healing only comes through faith, but it is a good foundation. It also just so happened that those who showed offense were not people of faith. There was no buffer or cushion between them and life's issues. None of this was measured intentionally beforehand. Faith is a choice. It is my choice but there are other avenues of healing that are healthy. If you're saying that you acknowledge offense as a need for healing, but you don't know where to start, here are some suggestions: You can first start by talking about it. As I said earlier, you cannot heal what you hide. Often, we want to bury our bones in a closet, but eventually you'll run out of space there and the door will burst open. Unpack that closet and talk about it, find a trusted friend, a therapist, a pastor, someone to just listen. You may be surprised to find that they have gone through the same or similar situation as you. Also, begin to process your emotions. Don't let thoughts and feelings revolve in your head to feaster and go unchecked.

You see, all I've ever wanted was for someone to protect me and to love me. To choose me instead of using me and then throwing me away. Like the toy at the bottom of the toy chest that was the favorite until a more exciting toy came along. Pick me up, put me down until I'm worn and you're no longer around.

You see, all I've ever wanted was for you to say I'm sorry. Just say it: sorry for hurting you, for using you. Pretending that I wanted you when I know that I don't. Sorry. For having you think that one day I'll love you, when I know that I won't.

As soon as I left home at the juvenile age of eighteen, I immediately set out to recreate the fantasy family that I've always wanted. I met and married the first boy that was nice and showed sincere interest in me. I liked him and cared about him but in all honesty what I really wanted was his family, specifically his mother. Not until now, I realized that I married him because I wanted his mom to be my mom. My mother-in-law taught me how to be the woman that I am today. Everything from the softness of my skin, my fragrance, how dresses fall gently and naturally on my curves. My gentle tone when I speak to a man. Still today, when I get up in the dusk of the morning to pray and worship God I sometimes think about her. After we'd pray and have coffee, we'd walk around the neighborhood and enjoy the morning summer breeze, we'd sing praises to God and talk on and on and on about his goodness. Still today I do all of these things. While I thought that I was looking for a husband. At the age of nineteen years old, I was actually looking for a mother. I was sincere in marriage. I wanted to be a wife and I wanted him to be a husband. I never asked him what he wanted, and I never ventured outside of the fantasy. He did. He did not act or do the things that fit my script, so now the problems come, and everything slowly unravels until completely undone. After my marriage the relationships that followed had similar patterns of me wanting the other person to fit a mold that I sculpted, the end result was always me being left hurt and confused. So, I decided to look at the patterns. In my relationships what were the common issues, was it my choice in men or was it myself. The easiest thing to do is to take accountability for yourself. You can't force change on other people, but you can change self. I was being selfish but in the wrong type of way. It was selfish of me to try to remake a person into who I wanted them to be instead I needed to learn who I was. Who was I in every relationship? The good things about how I dealt with relationships I want to keep while obviously unlearning my bad characteristics. The next time a new person comes into your life, friend, lover, coworker etc., be selfish. Think about who you are in that relationship both good and bad and decide in what ways you need to adjust. We are protagonists in our own stories, and we naturally think more highly of ourselves than we appear to the outside world.

You're reading this book right now but what you're really reading is my diary, a documentation of my personal journal of all of the things that I've been through over the course of my life to date. You'll see how my past affected my present before the renewal of my mind and the positive changes that came after renewal. Life is an exciting journey of discovery and recovery. Things don't change when you reset the time, they only change once you reset your mind.

Chapter One

<u>DON'T RETREAT GO BACK AND REPEAT</u>

I never enjoyed going back to Williamsburg, after all it has taken my entire life to escape that place. I left twice, once in 2011 to live in Colorado and once more in 2021 for Northern Carolina. Problem is, I've escaped the location but not the place. No matter how long I stay away every time I come back the triggers are waiting. All of the thoughts and feelings of the past come rushing back to me, like a heavy shadow falling around me breathing hot air on the back of my neck. This time will be different. I've decided to spend the last two weeks of the year here. I will heal where I was hurt. Yes, I've heard the platitude "you can't heal in the environment you've been hurt in" but that's not always the case. Sometimes you have to go directly to the source, don't just pierce the heart of the beast, behead it, that way you know it's not coming back.

The contrast of the then and now is beautiful. Allow me to show you how.

I was laying in bed today. No differently than most days, I'm deliberately quiet in order to see where my mind goes naturally, uninfluenced and undistracted. A hit song by Keith Sweat came on in the background "Make it last forever" My mind went back in time to the memory of me and my mother-in-law deep cleaning the house and enjoying the leisure of that day. If I'm honest, those memories have become quite common, so I tried to push deeper, to my memories experienced in my home with my own mother but my mind kept stopping short. As I daydream on, sporadically my entire body jerks, the kind of jerk you feel coming abruptly out of a deep sleep except I was wide awake. It's at that moment I realized that the love that my in-laws, mother (law), grandmother (law) father (law) have given me over the years have covered most of all offense. Over time their love for me has inoculated and overtaken my brain and my memories. The stronghold of lovelessness had been uprooted in that moment simply because a group of people had decided to love me no matter what and in spite of.

Not too long ago my mind was a hostile, poisoned and deadly environment. From time to time, going to long unchecked remnants of my old ways of thinking trickle back into my thoughts and behaviors but the truth sets you free! I am finally comfortable with being uncomfortable, are you? This time, I don't want to hide. The core of me is rooted in good not evil. Life's circumstances haven't de-voided my character and I can still be true to myself as well as true to others. Truth is. I've been so comfortable in my pain that now that it's time to leave it behind, it's hard. Hard to let go of something that I don't even want. A soul-tie with trauma. Rooted and grafted so deeply that it leaves a hollow hole. Embrace it. It's time to fill that hole with the newness of life. A deep breath of fresh air. A new stream of living water, not that stale pond that's been sitting there. I can't explain how much I long for a mother's touch. To be embraced and engulfed by it. Although I find solace and inspiration by other women in my life it's not the same. It lessens the void but it will never seal it. I will not forget to consider her feelings by oversharing memories that could hinder her healing. I'm not looking to shame or defame her. She and God can hold that conference. Don't be selfish with your feelings, don't let it go unknown that others have them too, just as much or more as you.

After my separation from my husband in 2018 I decided to "sow my wild oats" and do all of the lascivious things that I daydreamed about during my marriage, if I can be honest. (My husband was my first everything). I began to indulge in the life of partying and quickly became the life of the party. I love to dance.

*On the dance floor I was free, my body and the music
aligned. The beat bounced off of my curves and men were
encapsulated by the look of lust in my eyes. I was never sur-
prised when they begged with their eyes. The devil found a
way to creep in full disguise. I didn't know. I thought it was
fun, I thought it was free, I thought I had won. It's a part of
the process of healing, I said. but faster and faster my soul
became dead. After the party, after the drinks. carried away
by my thoughts, I would think. My head hit the pillow at my
home or his. The tears and the fears at my bedside they'd
sit. The morning after, the same prayer was prayed "Lord
don't let me die in my sins or mistakes."*

I had chosen at that time the lifestyle of partying, drinking
and smoking to cope with the loss of my marriage. I was

addicted to the instant gratification of attention and the fabricated mental release that came with being under the influence of marijuana and alcohol. What I didn't know then but can tell you now is that it drastically delayed the process. That was four years ago. Fast forward to now. I was in a one-sided relationship, my trauma of abandonment and rejection allowed me to believe that I was in a friendship that was growly into a committed relationship even though that conversation was never had, nor was there any concrete evidence of that intention. He'd never even taken me on a date. A friend with benefits, but that's better than nothing right? He'll come around, he's nice to me, helps me out around the house. I get the sin lead 'benefits" that we enjoy between the sheets. Oh, but also we pray together, go over scripture, we're striving, we are trying. Nah, actually. I'm lying, to myself that is. I just want it to be real so bad. So, the old way of thinking arises. I want to go dancing; I need a few drinks. The men find me beautiful and don't mind letting me know. So, I got dressed to go out. I'm in the mirror trying to believe the lies: I need a break, haven't been out in a while, it's ok to be bad sometimes, it's not good to be too righteous, I even said. lies, lies, lies,. but my mind has grown to a place where I can't believe it if I tried. No. I can't go out tonight or any night for that reason anymore. I can't delay, I won't keep delaying the process. It's time to move out of this phase called: Deception.

Your life has a theme. A thing that you do, a way that you think. The way that you posture yourself whether to your determinant or benefit. It's your nature. If your reaction is the same although the situation is different. It's your nature. Want to know the good thing about that? God can use who you naturally are if you submit that part of yourself to him. Instead of hiding from your flaws, acknowledge them, put them in the "to go" pile and give it away. Submit to Him and He will put the super on your natural. If I'm honest, I'm very selfish, and so are you. When people show me who they are instead of believing it, I war against it. Once hurt by something that I already knew, I blame them. There's a way to have a balance of selfishness and selflessness: Selfishness reveals your true nature while selflessness allows you to view the true nature of others. What comes natural for me doesn't come natural for you. What you do with ease, for others they complain and grieve. You are the main character of your story, that's absolutely true but the supporting characters help shape the story too. It's ok to adlib the lines in your script.

Even in the way that I plan my days at times. Rigid and routine. Checking off boxes on a list to the point that any deviation offsets me.

Even now, it's four in the morning. I'm up writing this to you with plans to go to work in three hours when originally I planned to write yesterday. Well, yesterday I didn't write one word. and who knows what tomorrow brings but instead of becoming frustrated about aborting the immutable way that I try to live (yet call it discipline) I'll take joy in the surprise of life. the path to a blessing is not always linear, how selfish of us to plan our own lives. A life that not only did we not give ourselves but cannot sustain alone. "In their hearts humans plan their course, but the Lord establishes their steps" Proverbs 16:9. I no longer thrive on fake love nor pretend that my exchanges with others are more or less than what they really are. That would be unfair to me and to them. I will no longer take more than what's offered or fill the blank spaces with lies that I've told myself while putting words in your mouth that you never spoke. Looking for love that has not been offered instead of embracing love freely given. I've stopped repeating the cycle of shame: dancing, drinking, and fabricating self-inflicted pain. I've pulled the trigger on my triggers and shot them dead, no longer looking at the things of the past with dread. I've redefined my nature, so that what comes natural to me is new. Don't retreat, go back and this time kill the beast.

Chapter Two

<u>TOO DIE FOR</u>

What can be done about thoughts of suicide? Why am I asking God not to wake me up tomorrow morning? Why do I want to speed my car into a tree? Why does my mind say that the blade of a knife would hurt less than the pain in my heart and a gun to the head isn't as bad as old memories. My life is better than it's ever been, I have small losses but greater wins. I'm no longer chained by impoverished thoughts; I've stored my thinking in the prosperity parking lot. Before changing locations I have to decide which of these lanes am I down to ride. Reach the destination that resides after pain or stay in this parking lot to die in vain.

Many a night I have come home freshly consumed by immorality and fully conformed by the ways of the world, but before falling into a hard sleep I'd have a moment of clarity where I would say, "God, if I don't wake up tomorrow, I won't be mad." Many a day I would come home from chasing the cares of the world: a business lunch, a conference call, a medical appointment, a worship service, and I'd say in my heart, I don't really want to exist in this meaningless life. I was quickly growing tired of going through the motions doing life without purpose or meaning. Doing things just because they needed to be done, all the while allowing unresolved feelings to go unchecked. Last summer, I reviewed my life insurance policy, just as a part of my financial responsibilities, you know, adulting. All of my T's are crossed and my I's dotted. A few days later, I drove to my nursing contract. I didn't mention that my career is as a travel nurse. My drive was a three-hour commute each way and it was a tediously unpleasant drive each time. This particular day, along the way the urge to drive my car into the trees clung to me and would barely let go. I already have a heavy foot and my mind kept screaming for me to bear down on the gas and let go of the wheel. The trees felt as if they were getting closer and closer until I was jerked out of the thought. Last fall, a regular morning, no different than any other. I got my daughter up for school, prepared her and walked with her to the bus stop. The hugs and the kisses were normal, "Have a great day, be a leader not a follower, love you" is my normal banter every single school day without fail. I go back into my apartment, brew my coffee and suddenly a desire so strong that it felt like it was physically loomed over me. It felt like someone put a weighted blanket over me that said kill yourself. I went for my pistol, it wasn't loaded; "If I shoot myself and die, I won't be able to see if anyone cares!" The knives! I'll just use the knives. I pulled every knife that I had out of my kitchen drawers, then I reached for my crystal Glencairn glass to finish the last gulp of the bourbon that I had. The voice in my head said just make small cuts, it won't hurt too bad, that way you can show your scars to see if anyone cares. Due to my foundation of faith, I knew better, I knew that the twins' rejection and abandonment were talking to me. I knew that my answer back to them had to be God's Words and not my own because that is my foundation.

"For though we walk in the flesh, we do not war against the flesh: for the weapons of our warfare are not carnal, but mighty through God to the pulling down of strongholds. Casting down imaginations that exalt itself against the knowledge of God and bringing into captivity every thought to the obedience of Christ."

(2 Corinthians 10:3-5)

I reached out to a few friends but they weren't available to save me, they had never really been available to save me. It's not their blame, they stumble in life too. Not to mention, me being the strong friend, they had no clue. I gathered all of my weapons of choice and hid them out of sight. I prayed my way through that moment. It took all day to recover from the decision that I almost made. You may not be able to pray your way through thoughts of suicide or you may not even want to but whatever you do, have a foundation strong enough that you don't blow with every wind or be devoured by every thought.

Thinking back on those moments and pondering why these episodes are recurrent. I realize. I do want to die! I want the old me to die, so that I can live again as the better version of myself and the only way that I can die is by self-affliction. No one is coming to save me; this has to be done to me by me. No one can kill me; I have to kill myself not physically but mentally and emotionally. I must kill the negative thoughts, the scarcity thoughts, I must kill the emotional instability, I must allow old feelings to die. Build a cocoon, shrivel up inside and in the right season rebirth as a butterfly.

You'd agree that there are three of us. Spirit, Soul, and Body. Most of the time we only indulge in the aesthetics of our flesh, our bodies. We're beautiful but our spirits and souls are anguished. Lately, I've been enthralled with the truth of my emotions and my ways of thinking. Is it true or false? Right or wrong? I feel how I feel so where do I store the feeling? I'm obsessed with learning who I am spirit and soul. Now, I ask you: Who are you? I can see how you look but WHO ARE YOU! Can I ask you something and will you tell me, or if not me will you tell yourself? Why do you numb your body with your chosen vice only to ignore the dolor of your soul and spirit? If you tap into your truth and then measure it against THE truth (for me God's Word) or measure it against reality, only then will you receive a glimpse of freedom and relief from desolation. It may be that no one is coming to save you, at least not in the way that you're thinking. Yes, you do have to save yourself, take yourself to therapy, if you've isolated, take yourself around positive people that you admire and look up to read about those who are hero in your area of struggle remove those parts of you that are necrotic to prevent the spread of death from you soul to your body. *"Finally, whatsoever things are true, whatsoever things are honest, whatsoever things are just, whatsoever things are pure, whatsoever things are lovely, whatsoever things are of good report; if there be any virtue, and if there be any praise, think on these things." (Philippians 4: 8)*

Chapter Three

I LOVE YOU BUT I LIKE ME

Sitting here in this restaurant, I've sat many times before. different places, different faces and with different thoughts I've explored. The comings and the goings of the people I do view. The backdrop of an empire, countryside, or mountain views. Alone. Subdued. Stranger but un endangered among the multitude. I find this to be true: I love you, but I like me too.

As I meditate this morning my spirit sings, "Arise shine, for the light is come! The glory of the Lord is risen, the glory of the lord has come! The glory of the Lord has risen upon me! I've noticed that my heart sings scripture that my mind can't remember. I looked it up and found it to be the saying of Isaiah 60:1. The living Word has begun to conquer the quest for ownership of the territory of my thinking. For so many years, you and I have lived life defeated and overcome by tainted thoughts, feelings, and emotions. Give credit where it is due, emotions are a powerful force but your feelings are only one part of your mind. Your mind we can venture to say is the spiritual attachment of your thinking but let's talk about the physical component: The brain. The brain is the epicenter of the body. The cerebrum, being the largest part of the brain, is divided into two hemispheres with four lobes within the hemispheres. What's relevant to our emotions is the frontal lobe. The frontal lobe is the largest lobe of the brain and sits directly behind our forehead. Its functions include: speech, concentration, problem-solving, memory, and decision making just to name a few. It's also worth noting that the frontal lobe is the easiest and most common area for brain injury. Brain injury can result in mental health alterations that should be diagnosed by a professional in that specialized field of study. The takeaway is that altered emotions, memories and decision making can be caused by physical damage just as much or more as spiritual damage and trauma. I've got great news! It is possible for the brain to rewire itself. In fact, most of everything about us can be rewired. My favorite fact about our body is that it promotes homeostasis which can be simply defined as equilibrium or balance. Trauma knocks you off balance but with intentional rewiring and reprogramming will can reach a place of homeostasis. You and I, we work diligently now and intentionally now to overcome that ugly beast named Trauma. Can you see how weak it has become? Do you feel the hero arise in you as you defeat the incapacitated version of yourself? We are rebirthing now into an area of healing called transformation. Let us search together, learn and dwell on some things that have substance and positive progression in our lives. Will you do that with me? We can live no better than we think, it will be nearly impossible to do more than we believe we can do. What it boils down to is: all of that, was for this. All of the crazy, terrible things you struggled through and suffered from but yet survived was for you to be right here to reach this point of transformation. Let's not be bound by the way that we used to see ourselves or the way that things used to happen.

We have a tendency to think that we're alone, that no one understands us or has been through what we're going through. That's a lie and a good one. "An idle mind is the devil's playground," too much time in isolation can become a deep well or a sinking pit with no one to pull you out of when you begin to drown. Yet, isolation is essential to self-awareness. The past two years I have spent traveling alone for both my career and leisure. Doing so has allowed me to enjoy my own company and get to know myself without the outside influence and opinion of others. My thoughts have been my thoughts and my view my own. Isolation has been my strength, to know that I can move about the world, functioning independently has taught me what I have to offer to this world. Knowing what I have to offer to this world has taught me my worth, learning my worth has increased my value, increasing my value has changed my circle of influence, changing my circle of influence has changed my life. Changing my life has allowed me to transform. A snowball effect in a positive direction. Remember the goal of me writing to you and divulging the things of the past to show you that if I can do it then you are more than able to do it as well. I won't say that I'm "transformed" because that's too final, I am transforming which leaves room for continued growth. There's confidence within me to claim this transformation because talking to you like this no longer derails me. I want you to feel this too! There are things that can be done during your time of isolation that are productive and progressive. Figure out who you truly are and what you like to do, things that you enjoy even if you're doing it alone. Listen to the thoughts that run through your mind when you are undis-tracted. At this time in my life, I take time daily to have in-tentional reflection, where I can be quiet and block out all "man-made" noise. I allow my thoughts to flow and my mind to wander. Are my thoughts negative, positive or indifferent and what is the root cause of these thoughts? Sometimes I'm able to adjust my thoughts after finding the cause and other times I accept that just for today, it is what it is. Also, I put a time frame on negative thinking. I say to myself, Yes! I feel angry, sad, hurt, betrayed by this situation and I embrace that, but I will only feel bad for 2 days or whatever limitation I set. After that time frame, those thoughts have no place in my mind anymore because I've rewired them.

Isolation can also build confidence. There becomes less of a need for validation, confirmation and approval of others. You become self-approved. Yet be mindful of staying humble because "it's not good for man to be alone." Isolation is only meant for a short period of time, it's never to be everlasting. It's meant for you to step back and find the beauty within yourself, the wonder of who you are. It's meant for growth, discipline and endurance. Its purpose is for you to look people in the eyes and say with all sincerity, "I love you, but I like me too." I used to love you under the condition of needing it in return, then finding it unreciprocated. I vowed to never love again, but to never love again is an ultimate sin. A sin that would remove God from within my dwelling. I like having him there, I like feeling him near. I love the light in the eyes of someone complimented. I know that I've made your day. Although a stranger, don't find it strange to return my wave as we pass each other a random person on a random day. Let God arise and take hold of your mind, thoughts and emotions.

"Two are better than one because they have a good reward for their labour. For if they fall the one will lift up his fellow: but woe to him that is alone when he falleth; for he hath not another to help him up. Again, if two lie together, then they have heat: but how can one be warm alone? And if one prevails against him, two shall withstand him; and a threefold cord is not quickly broken." (Ecclesiastes: 4: 9-12).

Chapter Four

THE TWO WAY MIRROR

I am she but she's not me, I view a varying reflection of possibilities. What has been and what can be are two different roads that both lead to a city that flows with what will be. The light in her eye can grow dim if I stray her away from the path within.

I liken my relationship with my daughter to that of a two-way mirror. In a two-way mirror, one side is a reflection of oneself from a first-person perspective without the ability to see what's on the other side of the mirror. Yet, the other side of the mirror is the reflection not of oneself but of the person on the other side. When I first conceived I was hoping for a baby boy. I wanted nothing to do with the thought of having a baby girl because I did not want a relationship that mirrored that of me and my mother. I named my belly the name of a little boy and planned the life of my seed the same. When the ultrasound proved otherwise, that in fact, she was a girl, I cried for three days. I did not mourn because I didn't want her, but because I thought that I was introducing my daughter to the ever-revolving cycle of brokenness. I did not want her to feel the feelings that I felt or have the experiences that I experienced. I dreaded that I was bringing her into a world that I thought would be similar to mine. I complained in my spirit so much and was ungrateful in my heart to the point that God spoke directly to me and said, "If you don't want her, and won't love her, I will take her." Needless to say, that scared me straight. "God, teach me how to make her life different and much better than mine. Teach me how to love myself, teach me to be a mother to a girl, a better reflection of me because I don't even like myself right now" was my earnest prayer.

As she and I have grown in years, nearly eleven. She has become what we call "my day one." She's experienced everything with me. The good and bad. She has seen things that she should not have and heard things that her years can't understand. There have been times that I've cried so hard and so long that when I finally dried my eyes and searched for her she'd be crying too. "What's the matter? Why are you crying Micah?" " I don't know, well, I'm crying because you're crying. There have also been times when she's come home from school and my smile and embrace didn't match the aching in my heart. Yet, she's never been betrayed by the mask of disguise. I'll later find her disheartened, and when asked her response has been, "I know you're sad mommy.

We've preserved and conquered the hurdles of life. This time it can be described as the busyness that comes with the increase of quality and livelihood. As expected, the dynamic of our relationship has changed again. Lately my enthusiasm goes towards everything and everyone except for her. As she tugs my coat tail with patience and wide eyes, I tell myself I'm becoming a softer version of my mother. I'm fostering a version of rejection and abandonment as I leave her to her own devices and isolation while I travel the world and venture here and there. I find her looking and longing for my undivided attention. Guilty as charged I notice and reprimand myself without change. Today, I initiated that change. I've just realized that our lives are a two-way mirror. She sees all of the possibilities of life in me. She's enamored, in the way that she tries to walk like me, tilt her head the way I do, her choice of words and disposition all a mirror of imitation and admiration for her mother. The approval she seeks, in deeds for my accolades and entertainment for my applause. Will I conscientiously reject her? Never! Unconsciously? Still no excuse. Today, I am responsible for doing a better job of making her a part of my world because it's not too late. When I was a girl, I mirrored the woman around me that I looked up to. I wanted to smile the way that lady smiled, my hips swayed the way hers did. Wherever I found the essence of a woman I was trying to capture it, bottle it and use it for my own. I can't allow myself to forget to be that image for my daughter. I would cripple at the thought of her searching for that outside of me. Intentionally I must be starting here and now. One thing that I've learned to do with my daughter is to teach her to live a life of cause and effect. First, what am I feeling right now? What caused it? What do I do about it? Due to her age and need for validation at this time in her life, whenever I give any criticism constructive or otherwise. She cries. I used to tell her to stop crying, crying doesn't solve anything. Although that is true, I was leaving out the most important part of that concept. No, crying doesn't solve anything so after we dry our tears, let's figure out a resolve. We don't like the way the circumstance feels? That's fair. Let's examine it and learn how to do it better the next time. I've also begun to teach her to celebrate mistakes. Mistakes are things that happen but are not definitive of the core of who we are. In my home we don't attach ourselves to our mistakes, we acknowledge them and celebrate because it is an opportunity for wisdom. Through wisdom, we will do it better the next time. I often tell Micah. " Your life isn't yours yet, it's mine. I'm living my life and I have a child as a part of that." You may not agree as my reader but I'm speaking for myself only. What follows is me telling her to watch carefully and observe how I'm living, the things I go through, how I respond and react. Hold on to the good you see in me and be aware of the bad.

In past times, I've looked to others for fulfillment as you often do as well. You have only just accepted that you can find it within yourselves. I'd be disappointed for losing out on an experience because it wasn't shared with others. Now, I've learned to embrace and enjoy the experience for what it is, not only with those whom I share it with. I want to teach this to my daughter. Twice this month she's been stood up by a friend who'd promised a night out for dinner. Instead of allowing her to settle into disappointment and validating that feeling I went out and bought her a brand-new dress and left a note for her to find when she came home from school. A scavenger hunt, instructing her to shower and dress for an evening out to dinner. I took her to dinner, giving her my undivided attention and explaining to her that it's ok for people to let you down, and when that happens it's ok to show up for yourself, by yourself if you need to.

Something else that I'm very intentional about are her career interest. Micah has a natural talent for the arts. She draws, sketches and paints with ease. Support of that from me comes in the form of introducing her into her industry. I take her to exhibits, art galleries, and displays. I introduced her to a formal artist, "This is Micah, she's an illustrator and up and coming artist." Immediately her posture erects with confidence as she looks to me to see if I believe what I'm saying about her. The goal is to build confidence, self-awareness and self-esteem. I make room to allow her to believe that she can obtain her desires by placing them directly in front of her.

I allow her to have opinions in the home within respectful boundaries. Growing up a lot of us have heard phrases such as: "Do what I say, not what I do" or, "Do it because I said so!" While it does teach the concept of respect for authority by default it also teaches against questioning and reasoning. Void of practice to question and reason, takes away one's ability to think for themselves. Without the ability to think for oneself, how can any of us make sound decisions? Remember earlier I told you that I surveyed adults to assess if they received the approval and authority desired by a father and the nurturing that they needed from a mother. The root of that was Need. Consider this thought. Just entertain it a little. Could it be that you should not parent simply the way that you want too? Is it possible that you should parent in a way that meets the needs of your child?

Respect is the least of worry between a parent and child if it's mutual with clear boundaries. Unconditional love automatically lays the foundation for respect.

"Train up a child in the way he should go: and when he is old, he will not depart from it" (Proverbs 22:6). What are we training our children to be?

In the two-way mirror of the life she and I share, she sees her own reflection infatuated with wonder and curiosity of what's on the other side. She doesn't yet know who she is, what she'll become or why. I have already been her. My view of the mirror has the answer of the results of each path. I can see the little girl, young lady and woman because I've transcended.

Putting aside fear of failure for her future is what I must do. First, I'll put away fear of failure of my own. I can say the same for you. It's too important to ignore. Your very own value is hidden in plain sight. Please change the reflection that you see in your own mirror so that you can give your child auspicious panorama. A hope that is real and a future that is bright. Let's not dim their lights. In fact, brighten yours so that it can illuminate theirs. We can all see clearly now; the murkiness of the dark is more translucent.

God gave her to me as a mirror of change and I'm not one to misuse a gift. Especially one too expensive to place value. If you want to know how to parent properly and raise a child, read Proverbs as a starting point. If your faith doesn't allow it and you want to know how to better raise a child, reflect on how you yourself wanted to be raised. It's almost guaranteed to make a difference.

Chapter Five

<u>The Wells of Isaac</u>

*The heat engulfs me. The warmth. I feel warm, relaxed,
even euphoric. I decided to embrace the feeling as my eyes
rolled back. Next thing I remember is laying on the bed.
Giggling, feeling playful and giddy. Afterwards, I'm told
that I passed out fully unconscious. My body jerked and
thrashed and my face twitched. I never knew it and I don't
remember.*

*Had I perished. All of my dreams, goals, and desires
would be meaningless and no more. So as we dare fix our
lips to speak of wealth and riches. First we must measure it
on the scale of what truly matters and what doesn't.*

There are many forms of currency and descriptions of wealth. My decision of being intentional with my style of parenting is an investment in my child's mental and emotional wealth. The culture that you and I live in says to "chase the bag". Let me ask you this question, in chasing it do you ever catch it? Maybe you grab hold of it from time to time but does it satiate you? The length of the chase and the strenuous effort makes you tired, doesn't it? Constant chasing of something that is hard to lay hold of and once your grip loosens, it's on the run again. What I've heard and what is now starting to prove true in my life is that financial wealth is of the least value in comparison to all other forms of currencies. Money makes misery and if it is your only form of currency you're doomed to be unhappy. I don't say this from jealous lack of never having it but because I have. When I have it, it flows through my hands and takes with it a portion of peace and a measure of happiness.

"Do not wear yourself out to be rich, do not trust your own cleverness, cast but a glance at riches and they are gone for they will surely sprout wings and fly off to the sky like an eagle." Proverbs 23:4-5.

Let's begin with the currency of health. If your body is crippled with disease, fatigued and ailing, what can you accomplish beyond that. No other form of currency holds value on your sick bed. There are so many examples of people whom their money did not add another day, hour, minute, or second to their lives. They could not barter or bargain for time. Possession of monetary value could not be taken with them. It only matters here, now and for a pre-calculated time.

While we're here though, prevention is a better investment than treatment. Take care of your body. Afterall, it is a temple unto the Lord and we are expected to take care of our temple. *"What? know ye not that your body is a temple of the holy spirit which is in you, which ye have of God, and ye are not your own? For ye were bought with a price: therefore glorify God in your body, and in your spirit, which are God's" (1 Corinthians 6: 19-20)*

Every day I invest deposits in all three of my treasuries. I invest in my mind by way of intentional thinking, cleaning out the storehouse of my thoughts; processing, keeping or discarding whatever needs to be there. Next, any form of exercise be it a brisk walk or a challenging run, the body is meant for movement. You've heard it said, " you are what you eat." Having intention with each meal is an essential investment into your storehouse of health. None of this is breaking news, nothing that has been unheard before, more than anything it is a decision to make for the sake of your own lives, if desired. Most of all I invest in my spirit. That is where my largest deposit goes. My time in prayer and devotion, seeking God for the decisions I have to make in life is what has kept me moving forward preparing me to face the conflicts of the day. Crying and falling apart in secret with him keeps depression and anxiety from taking over and unhealthy vices at bay.

Another form of currency is social relationships. Who are your friends? What type of people do you spend time with? I learned from someone special to me that I should never be the smartest person in the room and that your network is your net worth. Find people that inspire and motivate you. People that will discipline and stretch you, extending your reach beyond potential into progress.

Have you thought of yourself as currency? Around five years ago, I was struggling, mostly failing nursing school. I wasn't doing well at school because life at home was falling apart. I left class and drove down the street to a lake that I frequented. I needed to go there to cry. I held my tears until I arrived, checked my surroundings for privacy then let out a terrible loud and ugly cry. The kind of cry that makes your face distorted, eye swelling, snot dripping type of cry. I screamed all types of why, why, why's towards the sky. Then I moved to the walking trail to do what I normally do, walk the trail. As I walked a young man was approaching to pass locking eyes with me intently. I remember rolling my eyes and thinking to myself, "Please don't flirt with me, I'm not in the mood." As our paths came closer to crossing, we gave each other the obligatory smile and head nod. We passed. "Excuse me miss!" I heard him say behind me. I ignored him. "Miss, can I ask you a question?" I spun around with contempt. "Sure". He asked, "What do you do If you want to kill yourself, but don't want to go to hell?" I won't stay here long because we have already talked about this subject, but at that moment I became a form of currency. I needed to invest all that I could into that man. His life depended on it. After sitting under a tree for two hours allowing him to expend all of his emotions on me in exchange for my strength and encouragement, I was depleted. Remember, before that moment I was feeling lost and lowly myself. I was pulling my strength from a savings account that I didn't even know was active.

How can I measure your worth without knowing the price that you've placed on it? Decide your worth so that I can value it. I can't price that for you, no one else priced it for me. The deposits you make into your lives and the lives of your loved ones will determine the wealth that you feel in life. Isaac walked with God and put full trust in Him, he proved that by following the guidance given him as he journeyed. Every time Isaac dug a well he found water. When it was time to leave from one dwelling to another he'd dig again and once again find water. Provision was always his portion. His true currency was never tangible yet he reaped the benefits tangibly. Genesis 26:18-26.

Chapter Six

<u>Here Comes The Boomerang</u>

I bought some tulips a week ago.
They were not yet in bloom.
I sat them on the sill of the fireplace. A dark place.
I watered them.
I waited.
Nothing.
Days later, I moved the tulips to the dining table, a position
of artificial light. .
I watered them.
I waited.
Nothing.
Days later, on the dresser in the master suite, I postured the
arrangement directly in the light of nature.
The original source of light.
The sun.
Hours later.
Full bloom!
Jesus, you are my sunlight. I am a Tulip.
I've repositioned my posture, I've changed my terrain
In the right time, in the right place.
Suddenly.
I will bloom

What is love? Explain relationship? We chase the things we cannot find because our search is never defined.

Oxford Dictionary defines love as, "An intense feeling of deep affection" and also, "A great interest and pleasure in something." It defines relationship this way, "The way in which two or more concepts, objects, or people are connected, or the state of being connected." You know full well by now that feelings can be negative or positive. Yet, I've reminded you that feelings can be altered. I used to go into situations with anxiety of thinking, "Is this finally it, is this the moment, is this the one?" It put pressure on me and leaked out in an obsessively anxious way that could be felt by others. Now though, when I meet a new person, it enters into the newfound relationship with the excitement that comes from a fresh start. A new relationship with someone means a new relationship with myself. An opportunity to learn who I am through the person that stands before me –

while in anticipation of learning who they are as well. Who are you and who am I with you? Until now you and I alike have been in a relationship with Trauma but we've begun to sever the connection. Two different worlds in the same location. It was a process of preparation for me. First, I had to be broken so that the soil of my soul could be toiled. The weeds of the past were slowly but surely uprooted. I can't describe how bad it feels for the weeds to be plucked out of me. Furthermore, they leave gaping holes. You already know who the farmer is, the one who was pruning and purging my garden. *"I am the true vine and my father is the husbandman. Every branch in me that beareth not fruit he taketh away. Every branch that beareth fruit he purgeth it so that I may bring forth more fruit." (John 15:1-2).* (I've stopped throwing old dirt on the soil that He tills.) God taught me first who He was and how deep and vast His love is for me. I felt Him tangibly pouring His love into me. He is so gracefully patient in reintroducing me to His commands and requirements and how His love is so perfectly wrapped up in those decrees. Next, He taught me how to love myself. A year of isolation promoted me to look within. I discovered my true voice, and identity. Now, eloquently I am free to love, not the way I intended to when I first met and began talking to you but with a pure heart and renewed mind. Which means, that all of the hurt and pain of the past is no longer a weapon that I desire to use to protect myself and hurt others but now it's a treasure. I treasure the pain from my past more than diamonds. Had hurt not visited me, I wouldn't appreciate healing, had pain not dwelleth with me I would not honor pleasure. If loneliness did not devour me, I would not indulge in companionship. What if death didn't threaten to seize me? I would not be a conqueror of life.

The boomerang flew away and carried with it scorn and stain. I didn't know that its return would be unblemished, polished. Now there is a man that I love like I've never loved before.

The difference? It doesn't hurt, it doesn't waiver and it's not desperate. It's peaceful, calm and sure.

I woke up abruptly and looked over at you. Oh, the joy that filled my soul! It washed over me from head to toe. Each a layer of calm. A quiet storm. A resting place for both my heart and mind. Though my soul is not reserved for you, I'm happy to give you everything else. you noticed. You questioned the rapid beating of my heart. I was unashamed to tell you. All the while never wanting to tell anyone else. So this is love.

Chapter Seven

Queen Hadassah and the unfinished chapter

*I*t's shameful to bury my thoughts and feelings into journals and notes that I've written to myself. I feel an obligation to share them with you, though unsolicited and unwarranted. The idea of not sharing them with you nags me more than fear of exposure. If it's up to me to share these things, it's looking more and more like I will. My question, is it my right? I've earned no influence or popularity for people to listen to or hear me. Yet, my heart says aloud:

Who will feed them, who will clothe them. Unless you allow me, who will be the trajectory of change of my lineage. My generation. Without the hands that guide and protect me through my purpose like Queen Hadassah who was renamed Esther to be acceptable to foreign tongues. You took her from a peasant.

What about Phillis Wheatly, the first published African American poet and author. Whose writings and thoughts I mirror although we walked the earth in different times, paths never meant to cross. People before me who have come before me who had the same heart in a different generation. I've since moved on and the trajectory of my life has changed. Yet, parts of me don't want to forget the things that I have been through. I don't want to completely forget because I don't want the fighter in me to die, the survivor. I can't think to lose my conquer spirit. If I ever turn my nose up and downcast my eyes upon someone who has not yet reached their potential, my spirit will slap my hand to gently remind me, "You're never too far from who you really are" it will say. Whether it be my former self or my latter, both are my identity one in the same. Who are we really? The self we used to be or who we're becoming. I'll say it one last time for fear you'll tire of hearing it but I hope that the repetition revolves around your mind and takes root. It's common yet fair to equate the changes of life to a butterfly: the former with its darkness and limitations. The hardening then the vibrant release as the butterfly always leaves its dark place and flies towards wherever it feels like going. Never to return to its former self. never to return. In fact, if it returns that means it never actually transformed at all. From the beginning to now, I've transformed. I'm peeking out of the cocoon waiting to make my exit. Therefore, I cannot conclude this chapter. I will, though, start a new journal with a new title that will come from the voyage recorded in my journal notes.

About the Author

Ivy Gray is a poet who has been journaling her life's explorations for years. She is debuting her life's work and experiences through poetic writings and stories intertwining fiction and reality. She addresses her personal growth throughout the stages of her life: childhood, marriage, parenting and her foundation of faith.

Contact The Author

www.toowhomitmaydesire.com

Email:

toowhomitdesires@gmail.com